Collins

Treasure House

Pupil Book 1

Composition Skills

Authors: Abigail Steel and Chris Whitney

William Collins' dream of knowledge for all began with the publication of his first book in 1819.

A self-educated mill worker, he not only enriched millions of lives, but also founded a flourishing publishing house. Today, staying true to this spirit, Collins books are packed with inspiration, innovation and practical expertise. They place you at the centre of a world of possibility and give you exactly what you need to explore it.

Collins. Freedom to teach.

Published by Collins
An imprint of HarperCollins*Publishers*
The News Building
1 London Bridge Street
London
SE1 9GF

HarperCollins*Publishers*
Macken House, 39/40 Mayor Street Upper, Dublin 1,
D01 C9W8, Ireland

> Browse the complete Collins catalogue at
> **www.collins.co.uk**

British Library Cataloguing in Publication Data

A catalogue record for this publication is available from the British Library.

Publishing Director: Lee Newman
Publishing Manager: Helen Doran
Senior Editor: Hannah Dove
Project Manager: Emily Hooton
Authors: Abigail Steel and Chris Whitney
Development Editor: Robert Anderson
Copy-editor: Trish Chapman
Proofreader: Tracy Thomas
Cover design and artwork: Amparo Barrera and Ken Vail Graphic Design
Internal design concept: Amparo Barrera
Typesetter: Ken Vail Graphic Design
Illustrations: Leesh Li (Beehive Illustration) and Advocate Art
Production Controller: Rachel Weaver
Printed and bound in India by Replika Press Pvt. Ltd.

Acknowledgements

The publishers wish to thank the following for permission to reproduce content. Every effort has been made to trace copyright holders and to obtain their permission for the use of copyright materials. The publishers will gladly receive any information enabling them to rectify any error or omission at the first opportunity.

HarperCollins Publishers Ltd for an extract on page 4 from *Percy and the Rabbit* by Nick Butterworth, copyright © Nick Butterworth, 2005. Reproduced by permission of HarperCollins Publishers Ltd; Hachette Children's Group for an extract on page 6 from *Hopscotch Fairy Tales: Rumpelstiltskin* by Anne Walter, first published in the UK by Franklin Watts Ltd, an imprint of Hachette Children's Group, Carmelite House, 50 Victoria Embankment, London EC4Y 0DZ. Reproduced with permission; HarperCollins Publishers Ltd for an extract and 3 illustrations on pages 8–9 from *Arthur's Fantastic Party* by Joseph Theobald, copyright © Joseph Theobald, 2005. Reproduced by permission of HarperCollins Publishers Ltd; David Higham Associates Ltd for the poem on page 10 'Night Sounds' by Berlie Doherty, from *Walking on Air* by Berlie Doherty, first published in 1993 by HarperCollins Publishers Ltd. Reproduced by permission of David Higham Associates Ltd; Abner Stein and Simon & Schuster, Inc. for the poem on page 12 'Some Things Don't Make Any Sense At All' from *If I were in Charge of the World and Other Worries* by Judith Viorst, text copyright © 1981 Judith Viorst. Reproduced by permission of Abner Stein and Atheneum Books for Young Readers, an imprint of Simon & Schuster Children's Publishing Division. All rights reserved; Curtis Brown Group Ltd, for the poem on page 14 'Things I Like In The Sea That Go By Swimmingly' by Grace Nichols, published in *Asana and the Animals: A Book of Pet Poems,* Walker Books, 1998, copyright © Grace Nichols 1997. Reproduced with permission of Curtis Brown Group Ltd, London on behalf of Grace Nichols; HarperCollins Publishers Ltd for an extract on page 16 from *How to Grow a Beanstalk* by Janice Vale, copyright © Janice Vale, 2006. Reproduced by permission of HarperCollins Publishers Ltd; Bloomsbury Publishing Plc for an extract on page 20 from *My First Book of Garden Birds* by Mike Unwin and Sarah Whittley, copyright © Mike Unwin and Sarah Whittley, 2006, A&C Black Children's & Educational, an imprint of Bloomsbury Publishing Plc. Reproduced with permission; and Penguin Random House for an extract on page 22 from *Watch me grow: Farm Animals*, Dorling Kindersley, 2005, copyright © Dorling Kindersley Ltd London. Reproduced by permission of Penguin Books Ltd; HarperCollins Publishers Ltd for the extract on pages 24–25 from *The Prince and the Parsnip* by Vivian French, copyright © 2013 Vivian French; the extract on pages 27–28 from *The Helper Bird* by Anita Ganeri, copyright © 2011 HarperCollins Publishers; the extract on pages 29–30 from *Sam the Big, Bad Cat* by Sheila Bird, copyright © 2005 Sheila Bird; the extract on pages 32–33 from *The Lion and the Mouse* by Anthony Robinson, copyright © 2011 Anthony Robinson; the extract on pages 34–35 from *My Pet Worm* by Sally Morgan, copyright © 2013 Sally Morgan; the extract on pages 38–39 from *Animals in Hiding* by Charlotte Guillain, copyright © 2013 Charlotte Guillain; the extract on pages 41–42 from *Meg, Mum and the Donkey* by Simon Puttock, copyright © 2013 Simon Puttock; the extract on pages 43–44 from *Doing Nothing!* by Petr Horáček, copyright © HarperCollins Publishers Ltd 2011; the extract on pages 45–46 from *Homes* by Matt Ralphs, copyright © 2013 HarperCollins Publishers Ltd; the extract on pages 47–48 from *Time for School* by Wendy Cope, copyright © 2013 Wendy Cope; the extract on pages 50–51 from *Let's Build a Rocket* by Nicole Sharrocks, copyright © 2012 HarperCollins Publishers Ltd. Reproduced by permission of HarperCollins Publishers Ltd.

The publishers would like to thank the following for permission to reproduce photographs: p.27 (t) Ralph A. Clevenger/Getty Images, p.27 (b) Ingo Arndt/Minden Pictures/Getty Images, p.28 Anup Shah/Nature Picture Library, p.34 © HarperCollins Publishers Ltd, p.35 © HarperCollins Publishers Ltd, p.38 (t) David Chapman/Alamy Stock Photo, p.38 (c) blickwinkel/Alamy Stock Photo, p.38 (b) Piotr Naskrecki/Minden Pictures/Getty Images, p.40 WaterFrame/Franco Banfi/Getty Images, p.45 (l) J.L.Bulcao/iStockphoto, p.45 (c) Andy Hockridge/Alamy Stock Photo, p.45 (r) dbimages/Alamy Stock Photo, p.46 (b) Mark Richardson/Alamy Stock Photo.

Contents

Stories in familiar settings (1)

From 'Percy and the Rabbit' by Nick Butterworth

Percy the Park Keeper was in the park.
A rabbit came to see him.
Percy said, "Look at the snow."

The rabbit said, "Look at the mice. They're playing
in my house."
Percy said, "Mice! Please don't
play in the rabbit's house."
The mice went away.

Get started

Look at the story. Find the missing words.

1. Percy the Park Keeper was in
the _____.

2. A _____ came to
see him.

3. Percy said, "Look at the
_____."

4. The rabbit said, "Look at the _____.

5. They're playing in my _____."

Try these

Add your own words to each sentence.

1. The rabbit is _____.

2. Percy is _____.

3. The mice are _____.

4. The park is _____.

5. The rabbit's house is _____.

Now try these

1. What do you think the park looks like? Draw a picture of the park.

2. What do you think the rabbit's house looks like? Draw a picture of the mice playing in the rabbit's house.

3. What are the mice saying? Add speech bubbles to your pictures and write what the mice are saying.

Fairy stories

From 'Rumpelstiltskin' by Anne Walter

Once upon a time, a poor, foolish miller lived with his daughter.

The miller wanted to please the king. So, one day, he took his daughter to the king's palace.

"My girl can spin straw into gold," the miller lied, boastfully. The king was pleased. He loved gold.

Get started

Look at the story. Find the missing words.

Once _____ a time a poor, _____ miller lived with his _____. The miller _____ to please the king. So, one day, he took his daughter to the _____ palace.

Try these

Add your own words to each sentence.

1. The miller was a _____ man.

2. The king was a _____ man.

3. The daughter was a _____ girl.

4. The palace was very _____ .

5. The straw was _____ .

Now try these

1. Draw a picture of the miller at his house.

2. Draw a picture of the king at the palace.

3. What are they saying? Add speech bubbles to your pictures and write what each character says.

4. Write a sentence about the miller telling the king a lie.

Fantasy stories (1)

From 'Arthur's Fantastic Party' by Joseph Theobald

One day, Arthur had an idea.
He said, "I'll have a party for all the best,
most fantastic animals!"
Flora said, "That's a good idea.
I'll tell everyone."
Flora told the three pigs …
… who told the wolf …
… who told the bears.
Soon all the animals were talking about
Arthur's fantastic party.

Get started

Arthur is planning a party for all the best, most fantastic
animals. Draw and label pictures of the party guests.

1. Draw and label a picture of Arthur.

2. Draw and label a picture of Flora.

3. Draw and label a picture of the
   three pigs.

4. Draw and label a picture of the wolf.

5. Draw and label a picture of the bears.

Try these

Add your own words.

1. Arthur said, "_____."

2. Flora said, "_____."

3. The three pigs said,
"_____."

4. The wolf said, "_____."

5. The bears said, "_____."

Now try these

1. Who else will come to Arthur's party? Make up your own fantastic animal party guest. Draw a picture.

2. What will your animal say? Draw a speech bubble and write what they say.

3. Make an invitation for the party.

4. Write a sentence about the party games Arthur wants to play.

Poetry: The senses

'Night Sounds'

When I lie in bed
I think I can hear
The stars being switched on
I think I can.

And I think I can hear
The moon
Breathing.

But I have to be still.
So still.
All the house is sleeping.
Except for me.

Then I think I can hear it.

Berlie Doherty

Get started

In this poem are some sounds that can be heard at night.
Write a sound for each of these night-time things.

1. an owl
2. a clock
3. a fox
4. a mouse
5. a bat

Try these

Use your ideas to finish these sentences.

1. When I lie in...
2. I can hear...
3. I can see...
4. I can smell...
5. I feel...

Now try these

1. Draw a picture of a garden at night. What sounds can be heard? Label your picture.

2. Draw a picture of a town at night. What sounds can be heard? Label your picture.

3. What sounds can you hear when you lie in bed at night? Write a list.

4. Write a sentence about noises you can hear at night.

Poetry: Patterns

'Some Things Don't Make Any Sense At All'

My mum says I'm her sugarplum.
My mum says I'm her lamb.
My mum says I'm completely perfect
Just the way I am.
My mum says I'm a super-special wonderful
terrific little guy.
My mum just had another baby.
Why?

Judith Vorst

Get started

What does your family say about you ...

1. when you are naughty?

2. when you are kind?

3. when you are hungry?

4. when you are sleepy?

5. when you are fed up?

Try these

Use your ideas to finish these sentences.

1. My mum says I'm...

2. My mum says my sister or brother is...

3. My Grandad says I'm...

4. My friend says I'm...

5. I think they are all...

Now try these

1. Draw a picture of the boy in the poem with his mum.

2. What are they saying to each other? Add speech bubbles to your pictures and write what each character says.

3. Draw a picture of you with someone you care about.

4. What are you saying to each other? Add speech bubbles to your pictures and write what each character says.

5. Write a sentence to the boy in the poem from his mum telling him she still loves him just as much as ever, even though she's had a new baby.

Poetry: My favourite

'Things I Like In The Sea That Go By Swimmingly'

Jellyfish
Starfish
Flying fish
Seals

Dolphins
Octopuses
Otters
Eels

Crabs
Turtles
Weevers
Manatees

Sea lions
Walruses
Shrimps
Whales

But best of all
I like Mermaids

Grace Nichols

Get started

Find these things in the poem.

1. one thing beginning with C

2. two things beginning with O

3. three things beginning with W

4. four things beginning with S

Try these

Write a sentence to describe each of these creatures.

1. a starfish

2. a dolphin

3. a jellyfish

4. a turtle

Now try these

1. The poem is a list. Write a list of other things that can be found in the sea.

2. Draw an underwater picture including six sea creatures from the poem.

3. Draw speech bubbles and write what the creatures in your picture are saying.

Writing instructions (1)

From 'How to Grow a Beanstalk' by Janice Vale

Can you make a hard, small thing turn into a tall, green thing?

Yes, you can. You can grow a beanstalk. This is how!

What you need: a stone, soil, a bean seed, a pot.

Get a pot with a hole in the base.
Put a stone in the pot.
Put some soil in the pot.
Place the bean seed in the pot.
Add some soil on top.
Pat it down so the top is flat.

Get started

For each item, write 'yes' if you need it to grow a beanstalk and 'no' if you don't.

1. a pot
2. a flower
3. a stone
4. some pegs
5. some soil

Try these

Read the instructions again. Find the missing bossy verb (imperative).

1. _____ a pot with a hole in the base.

2. _____ a stone in the pot.

3. _____ the bean seed in the pot.

4. _____ some soil on top.

5. _____ it down so the top is flat.

Now try these

1. Write an instruction to tell people to water the seed.

2. Draw and label a picture that shows how to play a game of catch.

3. Write a set of instructions to tell people how to butter some bread.

4. Write five instructions that would help a new child in your class know what to do in the mornings when they get to school.

Stories with familiar settings

A. Write a story about a cat who got stuck in a tree and couldn't get down. Call your story 'Stuck!' Use the pictures to help you.

Instructions

B. Write a set of instructions for tidying your classroom.

Fantasy stories

C. Draw three pictures telling the story of some sea creatures who go to see Neptune, the King of the Sea. Write some sentences for each picture. Why do the creatures want to see Neptune and does he decide to help them?

Include different kinds of sea creatures in your story (dolphins, seahorses, and so on) if you can!

Writing simple reports (1)

Robin from 'My First Book of Garden Birds' by Mike Unwin and Sarah Whittley

The robin has a bright red face and breast, just like on a Christmas card. It looks fatter in winter, when it fluffs itself up to keep warm.

A male sings his lovely song all year round – sometimes even at night. He's a fierce fighter, too.

Get started

Find the missing words.

1. The robin has a bright _____ face and breast.

2. It looks _____ in winter.

3. It fluffs itself up to keep _____ .

4. A male sings his _____ song all year round.

5. He's a _____ fighter, too.

Try these

Add your own words.

1. The robin has _____ wings.
2. It has _____ legs.
3. It has a _____ beak.
4. It likes to eat _____ worms.
5. It has _____ eyes.

Now try these

1. Draw and label a picture of a robin.
2. Find out a new fact about robins.
3. Write a sentence about a different type of bird.
4. Write a sentence about birds in winter.

Writing simple recounts

I am a chick

From 'Watch me grow: Farm Animals'

I hatched out of an egg that my mother laid.

I pecked my way out of the shell with my beak.

It was very hard work.

Get started

Add your own words.

1. The chick _____ with its claws.

2. The chick _____ its little wings.

3. The chick _____ in the dirt.

4. The chick _____ at the corn.

5. The chick _____ in the hay.

Try these

Write one thing that you did...

1. this morning.

2. yesterday.

3. last week.

4. last year.

5. when you were a baby.

Now try these

1. Draw the chick pecking in the farmyard.

2. Draw you as a baby.

3. Draw you on your last birthday.

4. Write a sentence about something your friend did yesterday.

Traditional tales

From 'The Prince and the Parsnip' by Vivian French

Princess Sue wanted to marry a Prince. She wanted a kind and caring Prince.

Sue wrote letters to ten princes. "Please come and stay in the palace!"

Princess Sue pulled up ten parsnips from the garden.

When the beds were ready, she set a test. She hid a parsnip under each pillow.

The ten princes arrived at six o'clock. At eight o'clock Princess Sue showed the princes to their beds.

In the morning, Sue asked, "Did you sleep well?" Nine princes said, "Yes." Prince Tom said, "No. My pillow was lumpy and bumpy. I was awake all night."

Princess Sue knew that Prince Tom was kind and caring. He'd felt the parsnip under his pillow!

Get started

Read the story. Find the missing words.

1. Princess Sue wanted to marry a _____.

2. She wanted a _____ _____ _____ Prince.

3. Sue wrote _____ to ten princes.

4. Princess Sue pulled up ten _____ from the garden.

5. When the _____ were ready, she set a test.

6. She hid a parsnip under each _____.

7. At _____ o'clock Princess Sue showed the princes to their beds.

Try these

Which sentences match the story? Decide if they are true or false.

1. Princess Sue set a test for the princes.

2. She pulled up ten carrots from the garden.

3. The princes arrived at five o'clock.

4. All the princes slept well.

5. Prince Tom felt the parsnip under his pillow.

Now try these

What happened next?

1. Write the sentence that you think would come next in the story.

2. Write three sentences about Princess Sue and Prince Tom's wedding day.

3. Draw a speech bubble and write what the King and Queen are saying at the wedding.

Writing simple reports (2)

From 'The Helper Bird' by Anita Ganeri

This little bird lives in Africa.

The bird helps some very big animals.

Bugs called ticks bite the animals and make their skin itch.

The little bird eats the ticks and stops the itch. Ticks are good food for the bird. The bird also helps zebras and buffaloes. Lions hunt these animals, but the bird can see them coming. The bird calls out to the animals when a lion comes near. The little bird is a very good helper.

Get started

Read the information. Find the missing words.

1. The little helper bird lives in _____.

2. The bird helps some very _____ _____.

3. Bugs called _____ bite the animals and make their _____ itch.

4. The little bird _____ the ticks and stops the itch.

5. Ticks are _____ _____ for the bird.

6. The bird also helps _____ _____ _____ .

7. The bird calls out to the animals when a _____ comes near.

8. The little bird is a very good _____ .

Try these

Which sentences give facts about the helper bird?
Decide if the sentences are true or false.

1. The helper bird lives in England.

2. It helps some very big animals.

3. The little bird eats the ticks which make the big animals itch.

4. The bird does not help zebras.

5. It calls out to the animals when a lion comes close.

Now try these

1. Find out three facts about a zebra or a giraffe.

2. Draw a picture of the animal you have chosen and label it.

3. Write the facts in sentences using your own words.

Stories in familiar settings (2)

From 'Sam the Big, Bad Cat' by Sheila Bird

Tom had a big, bad cat called Sam. One day, he didn't feel well.

Tom said, "I'll take you to the vet." Sam didn't want to go to the vet. He ran away and hid under his bed. Tom found him. Sam hid under the table. Tom found him.

Sam hid in the cupboard. Tom found him. Sam hid in the shower. Tom found him. Tom got very wet. Tom said, "I don't feel well at all. I'm going to bed." Sam was feeling much better.

Get started

Read the sentences from the story. Fill in the missing words.

1. Tom had a big, bad cat called _____.

2. One day, he didn't feel well. Tom said, "I'll take you to _____ _____."

3. Sam didn't want to go to the vet. He ran away and hid under _____ _____.

4. Sam hid under_____ _____.

5. Sam hid in the shower. Tom found him. Tom got very wet. Tom said, "I don't feel well at all. I'm going _____ _____."

Try these

Which sentences tell the truth about Sam?

1. Tom had a big, bad cat called Sam.

2. Sam liked to go to the vet.

3. Sam hid under the sofa.

4. Sam hid in the shower.

5. Tom went to bed.

Now try these

1. Think of an animal. It could be a pet.

2. Think of how it could be naughty.

3. Draw a picture of it being naughty.

4. Write some sentences to go with your picture of the naughty animal. What naughty thing is it doing?

Fables (1)

**From 'The Lion and the Mouse'
by Anthony Robinson**

A lion was sleeping. A mouse was playing.

The lion opened his eyes. He saw the mouse. The lion let the mouse go.

The mouse saw the lion. He was in a net. The mouse bit the net. The lion was free!

Get started

Read the sentences from the story. Fill in the missing words.

1. A lion was _____.

2. A mouse was _____.

3. The lion opened his eyes. He saw the _____.

4. The lion let the _____ go.

5. The mouse saw the lion. He was in _____ _____.

6. The mouse bit the net. The lion was _____!

Try these

Read the sentences about 'The Lion and the Mouse'.
Decide if each one is true or false.

1. A lion was playing.

2. A mouse was sleeping.

3. The lion let the mouse go.

4. The lion was in a cage.

5. The mouse bit the net and the lion was free.

Now try these

1. Use the story map to help you write the story of 'The Lion and the Mouse' in your own words. You should write in sentences.

2. Draw your own picture to show how the story ends.

3. Make sure that you have written the ending, too.

Writing instructions (2)

From 'My Pet Worm' by Sally Morgan

You can keep worms as pets. Put some soil in a bottle. Now water the soil. Find some worms. Dig up some worms. Put the worms in the bottle. Find some food for them. Keep your worms in a cool, dark place. Check them and feed them every day. Keep the soil damp. Then, put your worms back outside.

Get started

Write 'yes' if you need the item to keep worms as pets. Write 'no' if you don't.

1. water

2. cheese

3. a large bottle

4. soil

5. milk

Try these

Which sentences are commands? (They tell us what to do.)

1. Put some soil in a bottle.

2. Dig up some worms.

3. Worms live underground.

4. Keep the soil damp.

5. Worms are long.

Now try these

1. Use the flowchart to help you talk about how to keep a worm as a pet.

2. Write instructions for keeping worms, using words like 'First', 'Next', 'Then' and 'Finally'.

3. Draw your own flowchart to show instructions for making a sandwich. Add the instructions.

Writing non-fiction reports

A. Write a non-fiction report called 'My Favourite Animal'.

Recount

B. Write a recount of a special day you have had recently. It could be at school or at home, with friends or with your family.

Writing stories

C. Write a story called 'The Lost Teddy'. Remember your story should have a beginning, a middle and an end.

Writing simple reports (3)

From 'Animals in Hiding' by Charlotte Guillain

What is camouflage?

Animals use camouflage to hide. Camouflage makes animals look like the place where they hide. Some animals use camouflage to hunt other animals. Other animals use camouflage to hide from hunters!

Camouflage in the sea

Stonefish look like rocks. They hide to catch other fish. Flatfish look like the seabed. They hide from bigger fish and sharks in the sand.

Camouflage in leaves

This snake's patterned skin looks like leaves. It hides to catch small animals. This lizard's tail looks like a leaf to hide it from birds and snakes.

Colour change!

This spider changes colour as it hunts insects so they don't see it coming.

Get started

Read the information about camouflage.
Add the missing words.

1. Animals use _____ to hide.

2. Camouflage makes animals look like the place
_____ _____ _____ .

3. Some animals use camouflage to _____ other animals.

4. Other animals use camouflage to _____ from hunters!

5. This snake's patterned skin looks like _____ .

Try these

Which sentences tell facts about camouflage?
Decide if the sentences are true or false.

1. Camouflage helps animals to hide.

2. Some spiders change colour as they hunt.

3. Some fish camouflage themselves in the sand.

4. They do this to hide from fishermen.

5. Some animals use leaves as camouflage.

Now try these

1. Find three facts about polar bears.

2. Write the facts in sentences.

3. Draw a picture to go with your sentences and label it.

Fables (2)

From 'Meg, Mum and the Donkey' by Simon Puttock

Meg and Mum took their donkey to market. Mum said, "Up you go!"

"Lazy girl, let mum ride!" said the old man. So Mum rode.

"That donkey can carry two!" said the woman. So Mum and Meg both rode.

"How cruel! Poor donkey!" said the man. So Mum and Meg carried the donkey. Soon Mum and Meg needed a rest ... and the donkey got away!

Get started

Talk through the answers to these questions with a person next to you. Use the pictures to help you.

1. Where are Meg and Mum going?

2. Why does the farmer call Meg lazy?

3. How do you think the donkey feels when he is carrying Meg and Mum?

4. Why did Mum and Meg need a rest?

Try these

Put these sentences in the right order to tell the story of 'Meg, Mum and the Donkey'.

1. The donkey got away!

2. Meg and Mum took their donkey to market.

3. Mum and Meg carried the donkey.

4. Mum said, "Up you go!"

5. Mum rode.

6. Mum and Meg both rode.

7. Mum and Meg needed a rest.

Now try these

1. Use the story map below to help you write the story of 'Mum, Meg and the Donkey' in your own words. You should write in sentences.

2. Draw your own picture to show what Mum and Meg do next.

3. Write a sentence to go with this picture.

Stories in familiar settings (3)

From 'Doing Nothing!' by Petr Horácek

The frog was at the bottom of the pond. Doing nothing!

She climbed on to a rock. She sat on a rock doing nothing. Hiss! Look out! The frog had to hop.

Then she sat on a leaf doing nothing. Miaow! Look out! The frog had to hop!

Then she sat on the grass doing nothing. Peck! Look out! The frog had to hop!

She hopped and climbed and jumped and … and PLOP!

The frog was back at the bottom of the pond. Doing nothing!

Get started

Read the sentences from the story. Fill in the missing words.

1. The frog was at the bottom of the _____ .

2. She climbed on to a _____ .

3. She sat on a rock doing _____ .

4. Then she _____ on the grass doing nothing.

5. She _____ and _____ and _____ and ... and PLOP!

Try these

Read these sentences about the frog. Decide if they are true or false.

1. The frog was at the bottom of the tree.

2. She climbed on to a rock.

3. She sat on a rock eating flies.

4. Then she sat on a leaf doing nothing.

5. Then she sat on a mat doing nothing.

Now try these

1. Use the story map to retell the story to a partner.

2. Now write about the frog's day. Start like this:
One day the frog was sitting at the bottom of the pond.
Write more sentences. Add an ending to the frog's day.

Writing simple reports (4)

From 'Homes' by Matt Ralphs

We live in all sorts of homes. Some are high up. Some homes are noisy. Some homes are quiet. Some homes float on water. Some homes have wheels.

Different homes

Get started

Read the information about homes.
Add the missing words.

1. We live in all sorts of _____.

2. Some are _____ _____.

3. Some homes are _____.

4. Some homes are _____.

5. Some homes float on _____.

6. Some homes have _____.

Try these

Which sentences tell facts about homes? Write 'true' or 'false' for each one.

1. All homes are the same.

2. We all live in different homes.

3. Some are underground.

4. All homes are noisy.

5. Some homes have wheels.

Now try these

1. Look at the photographs of different homes. Think about your home. Talk about the different homes with a partner.

2. Draw a picture of the inside of your house and label the different rooms.

3. Write sentences about your home and your garden, if you have one.

Information writing

'Time for School'

Time for school, so here I come.

Hello teacher. Bye-bye Mum.

Hello friends. Another day –

Hours and hours to work and play.

Books to read and sums to do,

Stories, painting pictures too.

When the bell rings, we go out,

Run around and laugh and shout.

Then back in through the classroom door.

We're quiet again. We work some more.

We sing, we clap, we stamp our feet,

And then, at last, it's time to eat.

More play, more work, all afternoon.

I'm tired. Is it home time soon?

Half past three. Home time has come.

Bye-bye teacher. Hello Mum.

Wendy Cope

Get started

Write five things that the children do at school.

1. _____

2. _____

3. _____

4. _____

5. _____

Try these

Put these activities from the poem in the right order to tell the story of the school day.

1. Books to read and sums to do,

2. Half past three. Home time has come.

3. Hello teacher. Bye-bye Mum.

4. More play, more work, all afternoon.

5. Then at last, it's time to eat.

6. When the bell rings, we go out, Run around and laugh and shout.

Now try these

1. Look at the pictures of the school day described in the poem. Think about your school day.

2. Draw pictures for each part of your school day. Label them with the time of the day.

3. Write sentences under the pictures about what you do at these different times of the day.

Fantasy stories (2)

'Let's Build a Rocket'

I'm building a rocket,

as soon as I'm done

I'm taking my friends

on a trip to the Sun.

But what do you mean

that the Sun is too hot?

Oh well, I suppose I'll just pick a new spot.

I'm building a rocket,

I'm finishing soon,

and I'm taking my friends

on a trip to the Moon!

But what do you mean

that the Moon has no air?

Oh well, I suppose I'll just pick a new spot.

I'm building a rocket,

it's going to fly,

I'm taking my friends

way up high.

But what do you mean

when you ask how it will land?

This rocket is harder

to build than I planned.

Nicole Sharrocks

Get started

Read the poem again and then answer the following questions.

1. Where does the child want to take her friends to first of all?

2. What is the problem with the Sun?

3. What is the problem with the Moon?

4. Has the child thought about how it will land?

5. Does the child find it easy to build a rocket?

Try these

Which sentences tell the truth about what the child wants to do? Write 'true' or 'false' for each one.

1. The child was building a car.

2. She wanted to take her mum on a journey.

3. She wanted to go to the Sun and the Moon.

4. She wanted to take her friends up high.

5. The child found it easy to build the rocket.

Now try these

1. Draw a picture of a rocket you would like to travel in.

2. Write labels for the different parts of your rocket.

3. Write sentences describing your imaginary journey into space with your friends.

Information writing

A. Write an information report called 'My Street'.
Include pictures and a map.

Instructions

B. Write a set of instructions for playing your favourite game.

Traditional tales and fables

C. Draw a story map of a traditional tale or fable you know. Add captions or labels to it to tell the story.